ANTHROPY

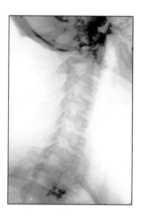

ANTHROPY

RAY HSU

A Junction Book

NIGHTWOOD EDITIONS

ROBERTS CREEK, BC

2004

Nightwood Editions
R.R. #22, 3692 Beach Ave.
Roberts Creek, BC
Canada VON 2W2

We gratefully acknowledge the support of the Canada Council for the Arts and the British Columbia Arts Council for our publishing program.

Printed and bound in Canada.

LIBRARY AND ARCHIVES CANADA CATALOGUING IN PUBLICATION

Hsu, Ray, 1978–
        Anthropy / Ray Hsu.

Poems.
"A Junction Book".
ISBN 0-88971-197-6

        I. Title.

PS8615.S8A67 2004   C811'.6   C2004-905081-8

CONTENTS

THIRD PERSON

11   Benjamin: Nine Epilogues

SECOND PERSON

29   The Almanac
30   Early Work: An Eclogue
31   Lag
32   The Art of Being Photographed
33   The Dream of a Fire Drill
34   On Trespass
35   The Room
36   March 13, 1957
38   A New Verse Translation
40   Many died.
41   Dora (Confession, 0:93 Seconds)
42   To This Bone Tambourine
      There Is Repetition But No Script

43 Pneuma

48 Our Master's Voice

49 Chamber Music

50 Midas

52 Meantime

53 Depth

54 Recording #8 (1:44): Excerpt from
   "A Natural History of the Torso"

55 Eye Level

56 An Epithalamium

58 Concordance

59 Where to Begin

FIRST PERSON

63 Anthropy

76 Olden Days

79 [Deleted Scenes]

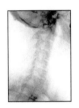

THIRD PERSON

BENJAMIN: NINE EPILOGUES

At
one moment in 1939, he extracted
an image of sharpshooters all
over Paris in 1830, on day two of an uprising
already running into the sand, aiming their
guns at the clocks on the towers.

the bullets
slamming into the clock face are a form of
dreaming, for sure;

1.

Benjamin crouched beneath the rotting metal.
Here, there was no such thing
as brick. They had forgotten how wooden planks,
slatted together, made boxes,
made brick. A city of wood could burn
to the violence of a fiddle.
But a city that forgot even brick misplaced even
crumbling. Glass too
he hid under, shivered.
Bombed out, discarded walls around him
blew finite rooms apart.
The entire place is losing its memory,
he crouched. *The city   the world. There is no map
that can hold a bomb.*
A light searing through the air
passed him. Stopped on the twisted ribbons
of metal across. Up,
he followed the long cone to the
Zeppelin, strange and lazy above. Lying there,
haunting the sky.
Through the archways jagged with glass
he watched the huge
static clock face jut into the air. Clocks, like maps,
insisted.
Benjamin watched it become
the slowest thing in the world.

2.

They say he started to forget early. First,
what things were for. Like corkscrews,
or Bibles, or fur coats. Next,
how things were, when someone asks,
"How are you." and there is nothing to answer.
Then, the way things fit together. With these,
wardrobes, keys and compound words. Last,
Names, the appropriate weight of each face.
Misplacing these was easiest. He could hear them,
exhausted,
leave.

3.

«Olá, guardador de rebanhos
Aí à beira da Estrada
Que te diz o vento que passa?» "Hello, shepherd
At the side of the road
What does the brief wind tell you?"

the narrator asks.
And the shepherd replies,

«De memórias e de saudades
E de coisas que nunca foram.»

"Of memories and of saudades
And of things that never were."

In this class, they have been translating these pieces.

One word has been difficult; it is at the centre of one of
their less complete excavations.

Sorrows would be one attempt, and has been a consolation
prize for the last half hour, and for many hundreds of years.
Nostalgia, meanwhile, something doctors invented in the
eighteenth century, is a tool like a spade, a word like many
from medicine, the only language to continue excavating
in Greece and Rome.

One of the students has been here all his life. He had been
terrified all that time of saying things.

Years and years later, he will squint. Squint the woman who sang into the smoky blue. This is a Chet Baker song that leaks into life when ironing, when rummaging through pockets for keys, makes him more addicted to cigarettes. Here, in the dark basement of the city, there is something that we forgot while growing up and leaving home. She sang about things we didn't have room to remember until now when, content to be the last in a line, we took to the nearest bench and sat down to watch the people go. He had forgotten about that   how there was a shirt he gave away to someone he might have loved, how he set an appointment to get a poem pinned on his arm   he chickened out but leaned closer to hear this woman this woman this song by chet baker   singing so slow she close to stopped   in this dark basement where he was   this song tell him why he was here and still alive   chet, who played
the blues
in his own way
he was fond of putting heroin in his body
he was also a man
who fell out of a window in amsterdam

The blues.

"What?" they said. They thought for a moment. "What?"

'Saudades.'

One said, "But that would be a different kind of word. It'd be a different kind of translation." Another nodded.

"But 'the blues.'"

'Yes.' he said. 'The blues.'

The professor, breathing, waited.

'Saudades. Around it is a thick knot of words, and deep within it is another word, written with the care of a slow hand, blues. This language never invented a word for it because it never had to. Before.'

They didn't know whether it was true. Saudades, one said silently, testing it out. Saudades.

4.

Nazi Paris,   where
the People become an endless film. The Revolution fist, on
the other hand, smashes down lazy doors and takes food. A
hungry man has a fist. One for himself and another for the
man beside him. A fist can feed a baby and can build a
house. A fist can be safe.

Take this shovel. It is the enemy of the ground. Use it to
write a play where the shovel appears at the beginning and
at the end. The people are important the shovel is
important. If a door is locked, use the shovel. If a man is
wrong, use the shovel.

If I should die on the floor, use the shovel to return me
somewhere. Do not use a splendid sentence the splendid
sentence is not a shovel. The splendid shovel is not a shovel.
Do not apologize you are not sorry.

Tomorrow I will be going on the trolley. I will not be taking
the train. The map I did not take with me said nothing
about a way to Spain. Do not follow me I did not take it.

5.

EXT. FIELDS, PORT BOU, SPAIN 1940. EVENING

The hills as seen from the air. The sun drags its long shadow across the hills, draining them of their colours and spreading over them variations of deep crimson. The mountains are far away.

THREE FIGURES are impossible to identify from this height. ANOTHER FIGURE follows, a fair distance behind.

> BENJAMIN (O/S)
> The Spanish farmer brings out his cows after sunset. In the morning, the mist is so thick that they low or else get lost and wander away. Or maybe they appreciate clean earth in the morning and decide not to go home. Either way, they are patient at night.

The one stops, the three keep walking.

> BENJAMIN (O/S)
> I once saw one walk over a landmine.

The one keeps walking.

> BENJAMIN (O/S)
> They are quieter at night.

6.

In the Pyrenees, he said, you can hear the loneliness of a bridge. You can hear pure resistance to soft insects in the evening. Go quietly: you may see where passing water unwraps the hard pattern of the stilts. Water is always unsatisfied, he said, and this is theatre, where the sound of water is the sound of all those hands in the same room as your body. Here, the water has such articulate hands that it can melt pebbles with its long-fingered tributaries. Where are you now, the water says.

In the Pyrenees, he said, you can hear how the long, curving kingdom of autumn leaves brittle discoveries at the bottom of a well, where light is a deep clarity like a shivering sabre through utter darkness. And all around, the grass takes the water's absence badly, and remembers only the vocabulary of currents, of departure, which is to say nothing at all, but still curls desperately around my feet. Go further, and you will see how the river dies, where the earth has rattled itself into sand. And you will see how distended cliffs starve hanging: so delusional they reach both up and down forever. And here you see abstract kilns haemorrhage, unreal like a shouting painting.

In the Pyrenees, he said, the wind is quiet. Circling, it returns over bloated hills under cover of birds, feigning God, it returns, in the guise of seasons, it leads you back, like the long, restless cord of a country.

7.

INT. GUEST ROOM, VILLAGE INN, PORT BOU. NIGHT

The room is lit by a thin shaft of light through the window. A few books scattered on the concrete floor with photographs as bookmarks.

INTERPRETER (O/S)
Dr. Benjamin.

BENJAMIN holds the syringe up to the light.

INTERPRETER (O/S)
This is Sergeant Consuelo of the border authority. He is responsible for the repatriation of those *sans nationalité*. He would like to know where you are from.

INT. CINEMA, PORT BOU. EVENING

The smoky grey of an almost-deserted cinema. A Charlie Chaplin film is playing on the screen. BENJAMIN does not turn to acknowledge either the INTERPRETER or the SERGEANT in the row behind him.

INTERPRETER
Dr. Benjamin. Where are you from?

BENJAMIN looks at the INTERPRETER.

INT. GUEST ROOM, VILLAGE INN, PORT BOU. NIGHT

BENJAMIN slides the needle out of his arm. He is disoriented, knocking several vials over, break on the floor. He sags to his knees in the dim light. The unbearable weight of his body sinks like meat. His body stinks like shame. His body lies down. It has not yet thought of a destination.

8.

I recall the last interview I had with Walter, though there may be some parts I have repressed.

G: Jesus Christ, Walter.
W: I know.
G: Do you realize that selling your books matters little considering.
W: Of course I do. Of course.
G: You and Dora don't have enough to *eat*.
W: I know. I
G: Sell them. I'm going to sell them
W: Gerhardt
G: for you.
W: I need them.
G: Don't you don't need them all.
W:
G: Listen! You don't
W:
G:
W:
G:
W:
G:
W: Get
G:
W: Get out
G:
W:

9.

There was the time
when he kicked open the abandoned door advertising
nightly performances
in a *jazzkellar*, local musicians who later died
but for now brought
the secret delight of people who danced revolution.
He tore the poster by accident.
But where the flailing step of dancing made love
would have been
Instead there were many boxes leaking shards of
paper onto the floor.
His trembling hands swung the door
back, fumbled in his
trouser pocket for a lighter and refused to stop
shaking, Goddammit,
picking up a photo and leaned it dangerously close
to the heat.
It was a woman, a woman smiling he dropped it.
Picking it up he squinted it carefully
clear. It was someone he knew, a long time ago from
the brothel, where she picked him first,
nervous and adjusting his glasses.
But the style was wrong. The style was too old.
This must be her mother.
Or sister. Someone else. The edges were curling.
He put the photograph in his inner jacket pocket
where he would not forget it
and found a half-dozen photos of people he knew here.
Most of them dead
but smiling.

With a kerosene lantern from a cupboard he brought
a dim centre to the room
and began the steady recollection of archiving.
Over the next few days
he hid among the remains of the *jazzkellar*
that saved his life,
these boxes, these photos, these lives,
as they took their steady place on the wall
with the help of some
tape he found in the same cupboard as the lantern.
The city,
broken with the kind of forgetting that
eases the guilt of going forward,
was thus rebuilt as a gallery in the small cellar
it hid so carefully. From box to wall,
the order was lost one photo at a time
until the aura of the lamp grew into the strange
faces of the people he knew.

SECOND PERSON

THE ALMANAC

It must be dismayed to disappoint so many
mothers and fathers over the course of this season.
Its simple miscalculation turns out to be communal
disappointment for those of us who had banked
on loyalty to our farm for another generation.
Still, it spares us the bittersweet subjects
like family and happiness, and dedicates its days
to all that stands between them. Because of its assertions,
we sleep at night instead of pacing by the many windows
that look over our crops. But even on its best days,
it does not have the time to watch my son return home
from school, nor my roof leak, nor the cows browse
the fence we have not fixed, nor the sky move attentively,
nor us choose one kind of life over another.

EARLY WORK: AN ECLOGUE

Waist-deep cradling
a shotgun through the wheat
reminds me of when my father
would push the egg
white edges back
to the skillet middle. I'd hear his keys leave
like pieces of music
morning would bring for miles
and the phone with its delicate
interruption long after he had gone
while I outside
alone imagined the tortured engines
coming home for sundown. Barbed
wire on the Derrick farm
brought every cow back
the way field
hands looked up and saw
the next morning. This time I hear
nothing, not the splay
of metal and skin. My father
turns to me with his grainy hands
as if his muscular face
could say
Lord.

LAG

I know you. The brown squelch
where your boot mistakes the water.
Behind the rest of us you lag
when you used to be fastest, intent
and fastest. By the time we grew to six,
seven, adolescent quorum, unpacking
our tastes like dirty crates, you
were long and lost, out of our league.

THE ART OF BEING PHOTOGRAPHED

When I saw my first James Dean
He was already dead. Already tragic.
The film is an extended funeral.
I fell for the race
He hurtled in. Left, against the door. Forward.
Did he also lean like that
In real life? Maybe he did before he died,
The car sliding under the trailer like a glass
Pane under a brick. How do you respond to a road
When the door is a heavy slab of metal,
Full of glass jigsaw, a serrated machine?
Signs lean like blank, stupid trees.
The engine is a heart,
A handful of nails.

THE DREAM OF A FIRE DRILL

The stairwell in the back
nobody uses. A bird calling
would descend, calmly
filling the centre.
Emptiness like this is made
through repetition: each step
barely fails to interfere
with another. Some steps
the light chooses.
The centre, so public,
is empty. It is automatically
formed of edges and says
almost nothing. But
the possibility of movement
hangs through this too.

ON TRESPASS

How the sun rises over wire
makes you think how metal can excoriate,

Pull tissue prosthetically back. Ankles
once cuffed now remind
you of your arteries.

What is this crucial vocabulary
except the trick of an edge
in a shock of dark

severance? Back & down
a steel toed sky: please.
                          don't shoot.

THE ROOM

Rewind the tape
and you will hear
their voices. One
of them flicks
the switch on so
they can see
each other. Five
minutes later you
will hear the same
switch because
they are running
out of power. One
of them is praying:
you can hear
his boots scrape
the floor. He is so
intimately on his
own but they still
lay their stories
at his feet. Over
many years things
went wrong. They
must have been
signalling overhead
for a long time.

My name is Francisco Gómez Bermejo. I have twenty minutes. I live down the street from a bar where the best musicians in Cuba come to play. My father would bring me there every Thursday night, when his favourite singer would say, My soul is so heavy / Clear a path in the cane leaves / I want to sit down. When I was twelve I started writing songs. I would write duets for her and my father. He would use his guitar to find the right music. I learned then that music could be so beautiful that you wake up listening to it. Those days were hard. I gave up school to eat. I would pass around a small hat for money. I started writing propaganda when I was fourteen, songs for older men. I will work so hard that I will reach the end, they'd say, and it will be over. I will get married and come back to the country, they'd say, this world is the most beautiful one. There was one verse I never wrote. How heavy are their arms? Our eyes will outlive them. Let us carry them into the fields they have learned by heart.

I carry my heart / to sacred places. / Oh, for your graceful manners / I fell for them first. Many of my friends heard her recordings and would bring them with us into the streets. When we learned how to die for what we believed in, she kept us company when we were alone. One of my friends could only speak to her when he had a trumpet in his hands.

When I was seventeen, he came to my door. "Come with me," he said. I was shining shoes at the time. "We need you." But I said, "I can't. I have to feed my son." Still he insisted. He reminded me of the days when we grew up together, the way that we would run into the fields and use them to imagine another place. There we became old men playing dominoes and making recordings. I would marry a singer. With her voice she could / turn wine into money / Oh her voice was so lovely / she would make your love holy.

What does *desaparecidos* translate into? What do the 'disappeared' sound like? Someone said that instruments cannot tell stories. But they talk amongst themselves, answer each other, speak in unison. And the song that I have written over the next few pages is for those who will outlive me. It describes a man who must decide whether to run from his country or to wait by his desk with a gun in the drawer.

The jungles are larger than we had ever imagined. How did I think this would be? We always thought we were pilgrims. We are moving flashlights along a road to the end of things. At the end of the story, we will return home. Growing up is difficult. But the hardest part is going back. This is what my friend told me with the trumpet he left behind and hid inside. He would hold it with a handkerchief, as if it were bleeding as he played.

ch'io vidi due ghiacciati in una buca,
126 sì che l'un capo a l'altro era cappello;

e come 'l pan per fame si manduca
così 'l sovran li denti a l'altro pose
129 là 've 'l cervel s'aggiugne con la nuca:

non altrimenti Tidëo si rose
le tempie a Menalippo per disdegno,
132 che quei faceva il teschio e l'altre cose.

"O tu che mostri per sì bestial segno
odio sovra colui che tu ti mangi,
135 dimmi 'l perché," diss'io, "per tal convegno,

che se tu a ragion di lui ti piangi,
sappiendo chi voi siete e la sua pecca,
nel mondo suso ancora io te ne cangi,
139 se quella con ch'io parlo non si secca."

La bocca sollevò dal fiero pasto
quel peccator, forbendola a' capelli
3 del capo ch'elli avea di retro guasto.

Dante Alighieri, Inferno, trans. Nikolai Gogol
(U of Wisconsin P, 2002)

547 | INFERNO XXXII–XXXIII

were spirits prepared for each course,
126   complementing the crunch of each pepper mushroom cap;

A NEW VERSE TRANSLATION

our bread-famished mouths watered over
the sturgeon-head pie with all the
129   cartilage embroidered with fish trimmings:

Tydeus carefully teased from the platter
a fried fork-full of Melanippus's dumplings,
132   which swelled hearty aroma in each of our nostrils.

"Oh don't you be so cruel as to relish
your inclination to devour all that; I'd hate to
135   have to chat myself up," I said. "Next occasion,

an artful pinch of lemon for each plate,
to tip this vodka mouthful to that clinking tune
no other kitchen in world could match;
139   each cognac-coloured expression is nothing if not satiated."

His learned solution burned with piquant
wit, while the generosity of his
3   look spoke whole recipes we could feed on.

MANY DIED.

La Jetée

Ladies and gentlemen
on your right you will see foothills
where your ancestors fanned themselves
before battle. A trick of the heat
but the trees are moving
like water. At night they would clean
the fruit and eat slowly
under thirsty skies because
this was not the age for keeping
food. Yes ma'am it was easy
to get lost then walking was an illusion.
Many small acts before war.
You may miss the colours
which are basic like fever.
If the enemy downhill
sharpened their eyes they would see
tiny entrails of plums lace
their arms like a puzzle. On your left
such things as the taste of iron
the smell of pulp
from their hands. The style
of poetry at the time was classical
and lean. Words to describe dawn
and blood rushing to your face
and god they
protected those   Keep
your arm inside the rail
please. Moonlight
was a later invention.

DORA (CONFESSION, 0:93 SECONDS)

Hard to describe how his body exploded
in the tub. I had pictured him a godlike enemy
and instead he was mostly modest, not
much evil. New, rare, briefly astonished
then he just settled back into the water. Fragments
of plaster hung. Disappointing how unguilty
he bypassed all those rapes, casual injustices,
impatiences, lice which slid off. Hard to imagine
the soft ticking feet passing as he finished
combing his slow hair around
his hammered look, flat. Already I was going,
already a slight depression kicking in. The flowers
on the sill watched.

TO THIS BONE TAMBOURINE
THERE IS REPETITION BUT NO SCRIPT

To this bone tambourine lying quietly in
A suit is a dried rind that at one time slid
Underwater it finds a tree that offers directions for
Rest from mimicking arms and legs allows one
To stop all the shaking approximate direction

To this bone tambourine there is repetition but no
Script in a mad hand our intention to render obsolete
All explanations are thin portraits that begin in this
Corner a crawlspace for which senses are awkward and
Unruly this sad scaffold this breathing instrument

PNEUMA

I

Inside pine gut, the marauders stood, tar-shrouded,
shoulder to shoulder in hollow ambush. Until
a voice lifted each of their names across the sea,

to their wives, weaving, waiting for beacons. Olive
deep columns that held up walls, ten years since absent.
Broken with memory, the men wept quiet in their bones

for this voice. It was that of all missing women.
Diomedes, Menelaus, do not lie down
and die. I will hold you back, though I am blind too.

Thus they were invisible, all but Anticlus,
who could not hold his heart, raising slurred fist to strike
pine wall. Odysseus struck him mute. All was quiet.

Helen turned from this pine nothing, for she could not
break a horse like fruit. The mute only take so much.
She lifted her attention, milk spilled on velvet

elsewhere. They were alone. No comfort from straddling
each other in closed spaces. They wanted to burst
like a heart into the sodden ground,

expelled like faecum into cities. For years tilling nothing
until their children were half-buried with boredom.
Wood was not meant to contain overflowing men.

Each dropped from the Caesarean gape of the belly
although only Odysseus still drew regular
breaths. He slapped the others until they saw again.

It was night, when they could cancel each other out.
They whispered their feet through the grass, far beyond wood
to stone walls. They had had their fill of air curdled

even by comrade. Just so, they looked for sentries
but found clouds, spare and drifting away like corpses.
How they mistook a roaming man for a sentry

I will not tell. And they would do nothing to him
except take his life, leaving nails clutching the wall.
That was how they disappeared like humble cigarettes.

A poisonous interval when the sentry heard
no answer. Silent city like a hieroglyph.
Moments before death things are more than beautiful.

Dust parted before them, left them alone, scrambling
to the sky, surviving them long after they left.
Doors cried open. Alarmed stood up. An arm. A leg.

This would not be recorded. Some were fortunate:
had windows, long streets before they died. Some danced off
thatched roofs. Distilled into the streets they learned by heart.

Achaean swords lit ten-year orbits around them,
inventing limbs and torsos as they went. Trojans,
hands empty, died. Wet and abstract screaming. Above,

clouds make love, shadows dissolving somewhere before
the baked clay knotted by black reefs. A brief, west wind
tints the air, bleeding into the ordinary.

Of the dozen, the head courier dismounts, bows low. His head
bared by the helmet under his arm is vincible.

Sima Yi leads one hundred and fifty thousand at double
march. He has taken Ye Gorge, and will arrive here by
nightfall. He demands you abandon your fortifications.

You receive this news gravely. Your men at Ye Gorge are pieces. You
have known this now for many years, visited them before their
deaths. Thanked them for their loyalty. Bowing again, he returns
to his saddle.

Five thousand men that you had not encountered in your dreams.
These deaths you had not augured. All you had to defend this city
against Sima Yi.
Half of the five thousand were to move grain and provender: Deep
kneed men trickled millet in grass for miles.

Two thousand five hundred remain.
You mounted the city walls. Indeed, there, the distant incredible of
dust clouds rising as two northern armies together. You turned,
high above your men

Put away all banners. Flags. Hide them.
Execute any man who enters or leaves without my
authority or who raises his voice.

Resolute: Open the Four Gates of this city.

They would not murmur for fear of you.
They disguised themselves as civilians. Broke straw into brooms.
Swept the roadways scared.
You donned a cloak of crane-feather and sat before the zither.
Burned incense, you played.

First came the scouts. They left, surprised.
Sima Yi laughed the way there until he saw it himself. Indeed, you
by the turret: crane-feather, incense, zither, smile.
And open gates. Commoners sweeping.

> *Swept the roadways scared.*

One hundred, fifty thousand retreated to the hills. Second son,
Sima Zhao, asked

Father: why retreat? What makes you so sure it isn't a trick?

struck for disobedience. Sima Yi,

You do not know Kongming, Son: he has always, foremost
and always, been a cautious man. He has never tempted the
fates. He opened the gates to ambush us, destroy us inside.
You are too young to yet know caution.

Thus they withdrew.

Far away, the men cast aside their garments and were amazed.

Why did a great general like Sima Yi with one hundred and
fifty thousand men withdraw at the sight of Your
Excellency?

You,

Sima Yi is a knowledgeable man. He knows that I am a cautious man who has never tempted fate. He saw me open the gates, saw an ambush, and thus withdrew. Now he will be heading north to the hills, where I have told Guan Xing, Zhao Bao and their men to meet them.

Thus Kongming, who never tempted fate, saved five thousand men with the help of a zither and an empty city.

OUR MASTER'S VOICE

The adults sat around their radios and cried. The children gathered outside in the dusty road and whispered their bewilderment. We were most confused and disappointed by the fact that the emperor had spoken in a human voice.

– Oe Kenzaburo

The seedlings we had planted
east of the village were on fire
the day the Emperor spoke. We
tried to put out our roofs with water
from the river. This morning
we bring shrapnel
and the unexploded to the shrine
to see them whole. We hear
him as a man
for the first time. Very gradually
we hear our mistake. When you hear it
you hear it alone. A father, they say,
is habit, a god who dislikes
disorder.

CHAMBER MUSIC

Try this: reach so far back into the mirror
that it describes a mythology. Each branch
strikes you as a melody, a method for whole notes,
Italian words that describe to the eye slowly
and motion. This is where someone was
when he, towards evening, found that birdcalls
turn wilder and wrote these down.
Later, a soldier hearing how insects offer
hollow sounds stubbed out a cigarette.
You are alone here
with these acoustics. These are words
for the ear only. This depth is where statues stare
each day they keep watching. Gravity feels a need
for bodies, for its opposites. So we have
come to count on *seize*, knowing the dark is
where things still go on.

MIDAS

It isn't the loss of taste
but that of touch, the crust
on bread, the skin of grapes.

Diplomacy has been for long
as we can remember an exchange
of the senses: frankincense

for the Holy, oranges
escorted from the Orient.
The sandalwood boxes hold

brief textures from another
place. This is the perogative
of the few: in times of famine,

bushes and trees are kept
under safe watch. Laws keep
the soil nurtured. A country

you will never see will make
ships for distance, contribute
scholars to your civilization,

send clothes, tapestries,
literature, women, labourers
far from home to serve

your glory. But your foam-
flecked lips will always choose
the disobedient memory

of the harvest, the milled
fresh flour, the fine
pleasures that last only

as long as the body.

MEANTIME

One librarian is not buried. When the sun
comes up she props herself up on one arm
and reaching down she pulls out a collapsed edition
of Gabo's and lays it to bask on the fresh threshold
flapping in the hard sun. In the first chapter
a man plays a growing trumpet much as someone
is doing somewhere now. By now the others
work the broken dirt off their earthly forearms.
She reads in the first sentence how
a man dragged and smashed remembers
ice. They gather madly. Their limbs cut open the hillsides.
One picks around the floor until
he glimpses a sheet which he lifts
to the man with the tasseled trumpet. Under his arm
it stumbles, falls back, regroups, and unfurls
a recognition that makes all the women and men
and children and every last parent stand. Ancestors
glance back and consider their massive volition. They learn
to speak through the strangeness of each other. They want
to trespass. There is still time to put words
side by side.

DEPTH

The heart is a bucket
for all things.
              Empty,
it promises to fill. Look
inside: the contents
are clear. Rainwater
will always be the last
of what you find. You want
to see the bottom. You
sound the depth. You use this
to float long enough
to get yourself to shore
by emptying these things
over the side.

RECORDING #8 (1:44): EXCERPT FROM "A NATURAL HISTORY OF THE TORSO"

A woman I knew: I've heard it said there
were more important things than
the muscles in her mouth. The slab
of thigh or the mould of knuckle, blood
tightened out. All this made her wide.
Me poor and dumb. Deep.

                          Sex, then.
Vocabulary so accidental, so
unexact. Only brute materials. And yet,
even viscera have their direction, simple
enough to forget under our daily skin.

She was hard to admit. Each word
was only violence. Instead of religion,
I took up photography. No picture
unbotched. The camera reminded
her of herself like a sharp knife reminds
a body of itself.

EYE LEVEL

Only two of the photos have both you
and me. One is blurry, the grains less
strictly domesticated. We lean in but the frame barely
contains us. That documentary afternoon had to

do with seeing the world again. We could hear
vines climb at weird angles. Undersides
of stairs. Strains of tired gears as they
tried to fit into the grand schemes of things.

Those scenes of you from my point of view
are not like those of us in third-person.
If you hold these at arm's-length, they become
clearer, as if to say even details

change, so that holding a camera meant your eyes
had to adjust to a new kind of light.

AN EPITHALAMIUM

for two

I have come this far
by your music.
You brought it in from
the room behind us.
It sounds like
grass by the road.
Furniture shifting.
Us reading over carpets
for years, hours.
You are me dreaming
habitually.
Your song is more accurate than
I ever imagined:
it is the horizon
the sun showing
me where I am.

The music is an echo of your body
I brought it in from the
rain, arriving behind us.
It is the mirror of your ear
your breath
the pattern of your steps and
you reading
to me.
You make me
silent with love.
As you read I imagine
you reading to me

about a park across the street
filled with our walking
and we are
almost imaginary.
It is what I am doing:
the song is more accurate than
I ever imagined.
Now it has another voice
describing everything that should be
and this morning is so mysterious
that it is early
and late
and describes us waking up
hints at later verses.

Another year and we are
huddled in a chair
watching through the window
things go on.

CONCORDANCE

How a concordance is a book that breaks down all the words of an author and lists them alphabetically, according to how many times they appear, where they appear. Shakespeare, for example, says natural x number of times. Milton says God x times and Satan x times. Imagine having your own concordance: all your words indexed. You could find out how many times you said love. Or yes. Or your name. And what it would be like to discover the concordance of whom you love left by your door one day in August. And what it would be like to hide it under your bed, afraid. And how long it took to look up your own name.

WHERE TO BEGIN

Before I forget, let me sing you one more, an old song: a true story from someone, and my memory of her will be the last to go. And though I don't remember most of the verses, bits of the chorus go well with guitar. But I know enough that I can make it up as I go along. It's part of a larger song made up by others before.

Once I had to recite something by heart. Do you believe it? I must have been young. And I figured out every line dies the moment after it lives. And breath its fitful resuscitation, but for how long? The last sentences are the first to go, but they will take the first with them. Maybe it begins there with forgetting the road home.

And that is the encyclopedia dream: the Epic, the Bible, the Shakespeare. The hope that one may contain all, so that a moment of saying can say all forever. And the comfort that may spare us saying something less than ourselves. And most frightening of all, that we may be real or imaginary. Or *and*.

FIRST PERSON

ANTHROPY

1.

Where to begin.

Maybe a story in which you return home after a long time. Growing up is difficult. But the hardest part is going back.

Think of a pilgrimage. What if you took so long that now, standing before the gently holy memory of your saint, you discover you have forgotten the road home. Beginnings persist: they are more than a mark of where we began.

A man who spends his time saving languages writes about reading. Writing, he says, has been around for thousands of years, but reading has been around far longer. Hunters depended on animals to survive. Before you the animal, its tracks. Words on the ground, in the sand, broken branches. But their author gone. If you knew how to read these tracks, you and your children might eat tonight. Even if you have spent your life reading, these particular tracks might prove you wrong. And so you follow them with nothing but a hypothesis.

Your tracks are everywhere. They have made your world. At the end is the most important moment—where you began—folded into memory, somewhere in the evidence of the world.

2.

Suppose Joyce was on to something. Take *Dubliners*: a series of stories, each centring on different people, which all end with their separate epiphanies. Then *A Portrait of the Artist As a Young Man*: a series of chapters, each centring on the same person. All end in separate epiphanies, but all of them his.

But what about an artist looking back on himself, trying to discover the moment of his creation? He tries to write his story and discovers that his memory is not one story, but many: they don't cohere into a single, continuous narrative, but are broken into discrete parts. And worse, he cannot be sure whether he remembers them correctly, or whether particular memories ever happened.

But each of these earlier versions of him, real or imagined, may contain his original epiphany, the beginning of his new world.

In some of these versions, he was aware of this problem. Some of these versions tried to contact the other versions. And what if some of these were imaginary and some were not: would they know? Or are any or all of these first-persons chimerae, creations of the old artist looking back? How do they know whether they are merely imaginary?

A Portrait of the Artist As a Young Man is a *Kunstlerroman*, a story of an artist growing up. But can someone write his own *Kunstlerroman*, an autobiography, without looking back and filling in the cracks? An autobiography is still a story. In other words. An autobiography is a *Kunstlerroman* in reverse, working downward to a simple root.

3.

Virgil was the hall cleaning man at my school. My dad was late to pick me up again and I was sitting on my lunch box. My leg was itchy and I scratched a scab off. Outside was raining. My glue on the ski man had come off again so I put his parts in my bag. So Virgil said hello and I said hello back.

Hello.

Hello.

You're that drawing kid.

Yes.

Yeah, you're good.

Yes.

Why do you always draw dinosaurs?

Cause I'm going to be one when I grow up.

Heh. Yeah. You keep it up. I used to be an artist too when I was your age.

What did you draw?

Oh nothing. Maybe houses.

My mom and dad don't have a house.

Yeah. Where do you live?

An apartment building.

Yeah. Me too. Which one?

With dark hallways. And stinky carpets.

Yeah. Sounds like my one.

My dad's here.

Yeah. See ya.

Virgil worked late.

4.

There was a time when artists painted only still lives. Maybe this is what she meant by "look at *that*," as if pressing against the canvas you could look through your cheek at the artist, mad with stillness. "Yes," I would say. I take her to the gallery often.

I was walking through a gallery once and realized it was mine. The curator told me. He, as it turned out, had been my best friend long ago. When we were living off-campus in second year I boiled my hand and he was the first to save me. I even forgot that, and he didn't remind me. He has had a patient face for a long time, I think. He got good at it because his father would level a rifle very slowly in the basement.

He told me that Henri Bergson was a man who thought a lot about time. There was Time and there was time, and it took a long time for people to realize that the second one might be more interesting. time makes normal things faster, like love, and slower, like minute hands or executions or leaky taps. time is what I got good at.

I remember doing something as a child which made me into what I am now. Being an artist for a long time you begin to wonder whether you have made your whole world by accident. There's another story in which the authorities found Dostoevsky writing for a student newspaper. They enjoyed blindfolding him, tying him to a pole and pretending to fire. The others either fainted or went insane. Dostoevsky's stories were different after that.

There was the time when my friend found me outside. It was very cold and I had begun to die. He reminded me who I was and gave me some food. He began to tell me the whole thing, right from the beginning, when we met. I asked him what happened before that and he didn't say anything. He took from my pocket the notebook where I wrote all about someone I took to the gallery. He told me about her.

Daedalus made his world out of limestone so intricate that he couldn't find his way out. Search parties were sent, and then he was banished to an island where the king thought he would finally be out of trouble. But there he broke open a gourd and found the skeleton of a mouse inside. It had crawled in and gorged itself so fully that it couldn't escape. And that may have been the closest it had come to loneliness.

5.

Drought in the city means that the streets crack.

The air has been thick all morning. Pedestrians are rare this early, when the cool clumps of trees haven't yet slumped over, exhausted. One by one they stir, either from nightmares or just from sleep.

The feverish heat is one sign that he is still awake. Even the night was merciless, each minute a slow sweat. Kept the turbulent covers back and away, this flushed heaviness.

Surfaces became intolerable. Nothing would relent until morning.

Tonight he kept his camera on the dresser. Reaching over, he snapped on the flash. A minute, and the rising hymn of its waking, air packed electric.

Against his belly, the cool metal back of the camera. He wound the latch.

Flash.

He wound the latch.

Flash.

This is the still life he understood: this would be his record of the morning as it woke.

6.

I left the window open again and now it's cold in here. So different from your place, with stairs so sweet you'd weep to climb them.

7.

I have spent a great deal of time talking in third person, having grown up as an apprentice to a craft scientific in its aspirations. It is difficult to describe history in the first person because there are many first people, some who have lived on to tell their first stories, many who have not. The craft of the historian is, therefore, to sacrifice his voice for the good of the many. We've spent a great deal of time sending people out into deserts, into caves, into woods, out into hills, out into the water, out of our cities, into arenas, out of ourselves, into the world. This is the way we become third people.

Did I say craft or illusion? I have spent a great deal of time at my window looking at the mulberry tree in the yard. Even though I can only see the side of it that it has turned to me, I still know that it is dead. But from here it has the temperament of the moon: *See this side only. My best side.* The other side is jealous, folded into somewhere else, a cellar of history.

It is said they did not find Thucydides's histories until they found the manuscript mouldering in someone's cellar. This is what I cannot forgive about history: its complete lack of practical sense. The survival of Thucydides was brought from itself into the world in such a way that its story forgot its survival. The Third Person is a kind of forgiveness.

There are stories of ancient vellum manuscripts surviving hidden in attics for generations. Living there for centuries, they had keyless locks for old stories, the only of their kind, like stories whispered into tree knots that have decided to stay. Like hidden bones dreaming of their old pattern in flesh. Then came the old women out of these houses who heard the call of the paper drives. And huffed away the dust of hiding. And brought these vellum stacks to the wagons waiting outside. Perishables.

I have written essays published in leading journals in the field in third person. These essays have been quoted in other leading journals in the field in third person. The third person is a tradable thing; it lets you wear my body and forget yours for as long as you wear mine. But I never made it as mine and it was never mine, because if it were mine, then you never would have been able to wear it. This is the problem of the first person: there are many of us, and we may never touch each other.

8.

Now we've gone underground. A favourite haunt. Above,
oncoming traffic. Roads scar nightly. How does traffic know
how slow things can go? Your eyes follow me down to what

I had been thinking. Chairs back to back. The floor shows its
geometric burns from configuring the table between us.
Bricks lean out, hold each other back. Say this place really is
courage. Say the thicker braid of the tablecloth edge is
courage. Say this one song now is a blow-by-blow replay of
us, taking it all on.

This song now reminds us we were once an inarticulate
room. My mistake: an afternoon tune like a lurid tongue
uncurling. Makes me more naked, this kind of sun. Turn it
off,

I barely say. Across the drowsy floor to your drink and mine,
another of the same. You'll keep me guessing, the way you
flick your cigarette. Room full, not of smoke but shades of
breath.

This is the moment lessons were made for. I still want to
face you and survive.

9.

The same day she died I had taken a picture of her. It describes how we sat across from each other one summer in Istanbul. Two glasses on the table and a cup in her hand. The branches draped with curtain and Christmas lights, which the photo has blurred into ragged constellations.

The detail is in her face, where the grains have strained nuance, the distance between one grey and another.

There is so much to throw away before and after a picture is taken. She began eavesdropping on herself and I only watched, expecting her truthful shadow somewhere in a long, unencumbered landscape where trees waited like long-armed children.

Last summer we had given to bees a pear that lasted their entire lives. Entire days with only the sound of them, imagining what would happen if we had given them honey instead.

"Look at that," she said, indicating with a tilted word the direction of the sky, the thunder a prologue, its barren monotone. Barely articulate evening.

Focus is a dead giveaway, when you decide what to grasp perfectly and everything else becomes abstract, like coastlines on ancient maps, far from the details of home.

10.

One question left, the one that kept you listening. After these many nights, asking was inevitable, and like all inevitable things, postponed. She had finished her story without your knowing, and almost immediately you wished that you had written anything down. "Suppose this is it." It was barely even a question. At least you meant well. Or was it, "Come back." Oh well. None of her is your business.

The worst of it is on the one who tries to recite by heart. Lines less memorable will slip, and eventually they will tug at the best lines, until the whole unravels and only amnesia remains. The last sentences will be the first to go, and they will take the first with them. Accidents waiting to happen.

What a shame. You had been looking for her all along because she was your grasp of history. A story with her stays firm. The best part was how, as she went on, the saddening of each story, so that the first coherent world became the one you feared the least. The stories that followed took a smaller and smaller piece off, each ordinary day, until each was uniquely gutted. But then loss is the gift of every moment, isn't it.

11.

So how do you go back? Suppose it's as simple as retracing your steps. Suppose it's not so easy, since one's steps point forward. Blinded by the oncoming future, but what can you do. Not look?

So maybe returning needs you to step back the way you came. How do you look back? You cannot see your steps if you are walking back to the beginning.

When all is said or done. Done means not said, said means not done. Stories are what I forgot to write while growing up. Now, looking back, I must retrace my steps. My tracks are everywhere. Which do I choose? At the end is when I began writing, folded somewhere into the evidence that is this world.

So be it. This late, my project will be to find where the beginning is. There is only one of us to find it. Now where was I.

A few years before he went my old man said he wanted to sleep by the side of the road. He didn't ask for much those days so I drove him out to the hatchery. "Farther," he said, so I brought him out to a long stretch of 94. After an hour and fifteen I said, "Okay dad. This is getting silly." He didn't move. A real old Chevy ignored us half an hour later. We heard its axles go.

I gave up crouching and sat down with my elbows to my knees in the road's vast margins. The wind strummed the thin gold heads of the stalks. "When I was fifteen I got hepatitis." There were a few unastonished things I could have said. Like, Uh huh? Or, Dad, remind me to get gas. Or, Dad, it's getting cold. "Yes," I said. He was always the kind of man who said things that were not meant for me. Sons learn this the usual way. A father's privacy is no place for parties.

"I was still living in Lima at the time. That October I threw up on the way home from school. I remember my mouth was suddenly full." Most of the day he sits in his chair like a bag of cement. That I can handle. "I tried to swallow everything down but it just burst out again," he said. "I leaned against the wall, looked at the vomit around my feet and retched something clear and sticky." I wanted him to tell me this over coffee, where the passing waitress slaps the bill on a metal spike on the table. "A woman found me and pulled me by the arm to a sink in a courtyard. She washed my hand and then cupped her hands and threw water into my face. Then she picked up one pail, had me pick up the other, and threw the water so that it washed the vomit into the gutter. Then she saw me crying. 'Hey kid,' she said. 'Hey look.' When she took me in her arms, I could smell her sweat and the sourness of my breath. I didn't know where to look. I found out later she lived a few floors up from the courtyard. But I didn't know her name.

"When I went to visit her in February, she put the flowers my mother gave me in the window vase. She began to iron. The way she flattened the cloth, lifted the iron, set it down, and then folded the laundry was an exercise in slow concentration. 'Wait,' she said as I got up to go. 'I have to go out too, and I'll go with you.' She changed her clothes in another room. The door was open a crack. Two stockings hung over the chair. She gathered one into a roll in her hand, then balanced on one leg as she rested her other heel against her knee, leaned forward, slipped the rolled-up stocking over the tip of her foot, put her foot on the chair as she smoothed the stocking up over her calf, knee and thigh, then bent to one side as she clipped the stocking to the garter belt and took her foot off the chair.

"She felt me looking. As she reached for the other stocking, she paused, turned towards the door and looked straight at me. I can't describe the look. I realized my face was burning. I ran out of the apartment, down the stairs and into the street.

"I didn't return home for hours. Why couldn't I take my eyes off her? She had a much stronger, more voluptuous body than the girls I liked. Over thirty? Being my age it was hard to guess. It wasn't just her body, I found out years later, but the way she moved. My girlfriends didn't understand why I asked them to put on stockings. When they did, they did it as a come-on. They thought it was about garters and high heels and that sort of thing. But it was more like she had withdrawn into her body, unbothered by the world. Nothing to do with breasts and hips and legs."

He was quiet for a long time. Our car reflected some headlights as they went by. Dad, you've never been to Lima. I'm not sure whether I actually said this. "Maybe we should go back there this summer," I said.

I watched the sentence walk out and sit down beside us. The sky waited. "The ground is warmer than I thought," he said.

When I agreed to work on this project
with Carleton, I had a vision of the
whole. The opening sequence plays
much more like a love story in the
final cut. I fought to keep the original
scene order as well as Walter's voice-
over. See, here he is just arriving in
Port Bou, but he doesn't know it yet.
We just get to see the water, endless
water, and silence. He's just a speck at
this angle, we can barely tell him apart
from all the others who have stopped
looking out over the rails, across the
water. We were lucky enough to get
low enough to get the detail of the
people, so they could be distinguished.
At this angle and maybe it's a trick of
the light but the waves look alive, like
bodies pressed together. And this is
when we barely even notice the
singing. We hear it, but it's meant to
be in Walter's head like fore-
shadowing. It's what Dora sings later
on their last night. But nothing like
the way we hear it now: she sings it
under her breath, barely under the
crickets. He almost hears it both times
but he doesn't end up hearing it either
time. He thinks he's nowhere: once on
the bridge in the middle of water, the

second in the car with Dora at night. This is where we cut to nightfall, when everything slows down. In this version we go directly to when Walter and Dora meet. We skip the part when she drops an armload of books down the damaged stairs. One is Italian. She picks this one up last and puts it on top. What book it is makes sense when later Dade sees her learning Italian. It's to read the book. And when he has to teach her to dance, it's to keep her from learning Italian, from meeting Walter in the first place. All this way, her husband and her are countries apart, and that's why Dade is addicted to her. For him it's torture, he wants to belong to her. His scenes are shot in a filter that makes everything hot, so you see things through his own eyes. He makes everything around him horrible. But only we can see the whole picture: that no one in the story knows who they will fall in love with. They think they understand how it all fits together. We get hints, impressions, like when Dora crosses the street. The traffic is mad. Walter is still trying to cross the first set of cars. We see him through all of them as they rush by. We somewhat see her in the foreground, but our focus is on him. Something is going to happen, just as Walter knows something is going to happen. When we see her from his point of view, we see her with our own eyes. Something is going to happen, but we don't see it and he isn't there when it happens. He says this later to Quentin, who sits through the whole thing. Don't forget Quentin is also a patient: we're not sure how he got there or whether they're just sharing stories just because. But that's the interesting part: Quentin must have his own story (which we hint at in the final scene) but we never learn it. Maybe Quentin had had something to do with Walter before or even with Dora. But all he does is keep turning a watch slowly in his hands and listen. I wanted to point out how they all connect in ways they don't even know. But there's so much that's left out. I would have let them go on.

NOTES

"Benjamin: Nine Epilogues": ¶ The epigraph is drawn from T.J. Clark's review of *The Arcades Project* in the *London Review of Books*, 22 June 2000. ¶ The lines in Portuguese are drawn from Alberto Caeiro / Fernando Pessoa's *O Guardador de Rebanhos*. ¶ Some of the descriptions of Chet Baker are drawn from a personal letter by Justin Rutledge.

"A New Verse Translation": ¶ The text of Dante's *Inferno* is from Mark Musa's Indiana University Press edition.

"Anthropy": ¶ The "man who spends his time saving languages" is J. Edward Chamberlin. ¶ Alexis de Toucqueville writes about the mouse in the gourd, but the reference is lost; thanks to Sophie Levy for drawing this to my attention.

"Olden Days": ¶ Quoted sections are distilled from Bernhard Schlink's *The Reader*, translated by Carol Brown Janeway.

ACKNOWLEDGEMENTS

Versions of these poems have appeared in *Fence, The Fiddlehead, Echolocation, Pan del Muerto, Exile* and *The Hart House Review*, as well as in a chapbook from Junction Books. Some were anthologized in *Breathing Fire 2: Canada's New Poets*. Thanks to the editors.

I have benefited immensely from fine readers at The Algonquin Square Table, the Catacombs workshop, House of Other, Nightwood Editions, Premiere Generation Ink, the Vic poets, and the University of Wisconsin-Madison. I owe others for their advice and support, especially Quan Barry, A. F. Moritz, and Ronald Wallace.

With this book, I am especially indebted to my editor, Carleton Wilson, for devoting such close attention to the poems. I owe other debts to my family.

Bonnie Jean Michalski

ABOUT THE AUTHOR

Ray Hsu grew up in Toronto and is completing his Ph.D. at the University of Wisconsin-Madison.

A Junction Book

Typeset in TEFF Collis

TEFF Collis was designed in 1993 by Christoph Noordzij for The Enschedé Font Foundry.

Printed and bound in Canada

EDITOR FOR THE PRESS
Carleton Wilson

COPY EDITOR
Silas White

TYPESETTING
Carleton Wilson

COVER DESIGN
Carleton Wilson

COVER IMAGE
Nestor Quezada based on an x-ray of Tim Elkins
X-ray copyright © Tim Elkins, used with permission

Junction Books
568 Indian Grove · Toronto, ON · M6P 2J4
www.junctionbooks.com

Nightwood Editions
www.nightwoodeditions.com